The
Penguin

Published by Raintree Steck-Vaughn Publishers, an imprint of Steck-Vaughn Company.

Acknowledgments
Project Editor: Pam Wells
Design Manager: Joyce Spicer
Editor: Sabrina Crewe
Designers: Ian Winton and Steve Prosser
Consultant: Michael Chinery
Illustrator: Malcolm Ellis
Electronic Cover Production: Alan Klemp
Additional Electronic Production: Scott Melcer
Photography credits on page 32

Planned and produced by The Creative Publishing Company

Library of Congress Cataloging-in-Publication Data
Crewe, Sabrina
    The penguin / Sabrina Crewe ; [illustrator, Malcolm Ellis].
       p.   cm. — (Life cycles)
    Includes index.
    Summary: Provides an introduction to the life cycle, physical characteristics, behavior, and habitat of a penguin.
    ISBN 0-8172-4379-8
    1. Penguins — Juvenile literature.   2. Penguins — Life cycles — Juvenile literature. 3. Emperor penguin — Juvenile literature.   4. Emperor penguin — Life cycles — Juvenile literature. [1. Emperor penguin. 2. Penguins] I. Ellis, Malcolm, ill. II. Title. III. Series: Crewe, Sabrina. Life cycles.
QL696.S473C74 1998
598.47 — dc21   96-53248
                                                  CIP   AC

      4 5 6 7 8 9 0 LB 01 00 99
Printed and bound in the United States of America.

Words explained in the glossary appear in **bold** the first time they are used in the text.

LIFE CYCLES

The
Penguin

Sabrina Crewe

RSVP
RAINTREE
STECK-VAUGHN
P U B L I S H E R S
The Steck-Vaughn Company

Austin, Texas

The penguins are at the rookery.

Many penguins are gathering at the **rookery**. It is the beginning of winter in **Antarctica**, which is the coldest part of the world. Even the ocean is starting to freeze.

There are no trees or plants at the rookery. The penguins cannot make nests. The mother penguins lay their eggs on the ice.

The father penguin has taken the egg.

The mother penguin passes the egg to her partner. The father penguin tucks it in a fold of skin above his feet. His body and the feathers on it will keep the egg warm.

The mother penguin goes to the ocean.

The mother penguin has left the rookery. She travels many miles across the ice to get back to the open ocean. There she will find some food. Penguins eat fish and **squid** that live in the ocean.

The father penguin looks after the egg.

The father penguin keeps the egg warm and safe for two months. He has had no food since he left the ocean. He has to live on the fat inside his body.

The penguins are cold.

It is dark most of the time, and the wind is freezing cold. The father penguins huddle together to keep warm. They take turns being on the outside of the group where it is coldest.

The chick has hatched from the egg.

After two months, the egg starts to crack.
The baby penguin pecks its way through
the shell. A baby penguin is called a
chick. When it has **hatched**, the chick
stays on its father's feet to keep warm.
It would quickly die if it fell on the ice.

The mother penguin is calling.

The mother penguin has returned to the rookery. She gives a special call. Her partner knows her call and answers her. She finds him among thousands of other penguins.

The father penguin is hungry.

The father penguin has passed the chick to his partner. Now he is going to the ocean. The father penguin is tired and thin after going so long without eating. It is his turn to leave the rookery and find some food.

The mother penguin feeds her chick.

Now the chick is on the mother penguin's feet. The mother has come back with food. She feeds her chick with the food stored in her **crop**.

The chick stays on its mother's feet.

The mother penguin keeps the chick warm. She feeds it from her crop whenever it is hungry. The chick is growing fast.

The chick is passed to the father penguin.

The father penguin has come back from the ocean. The mother passes the chick to him again. The father must get the chick onto his feet very quickly so that it doesn't freeze. Now he will feed the chick for a while.

The chick is seven weeks old.

Now the chick has grown too big to sit on its parents' feet. The mother and father penguins still take turns bringing food for the chick from the ocean. They don't have as far to go now. The ice is beginning to melt, and the open water has come closer to the rookery.

The chicks huddle together.

The chicks stay close together so they can keep each other warm. Their fluffy feathers help to keep the heat in. The chicks stay in their group except when their parents call them for feeding. Each chick knows its parents' special call.

The young penguins have new feathers.

When the chicks are about five months old,
they lose their fluffy gray feathers. They start
to grow a new coat of stiff, black and white
feathers. Their new feathers are waterproof.

The adult penguins are hunting for food.

By summer, the young penguins are big enough
to look after themselves. The parents leave them
at the rookery and go to their **feeding ground.**
They find plenty of food in the ocean.

The young penguin is getting hungry.

The young penguin needs to feed itself now that its parents have gone. There is no food at the rookery, so it must go to the ocean. With its new feathers, the young penguin is ready to go into the water.

The penguin can dive deep.

The penguin can go as deep as 870 feet (265 m) when it dives for food. It can hold its breath and stay under the water for a long time. The penguin chases fish and squid, and catches them with its sharp bill.

The whale is hunting for penguins.

While penguins are at their feeding ground, they are sometimes attacked by **predators**. Killer whales and leopard seals **prey** on penguins feeding in the ocean. If a killer whale comes near, the penguin leaps out of the water and back onto land.

The penguins slide along on their bellies.

At the end of summer, the penguins travel back to the rookery. Sometimes they push themselves along on their bellies. The adult penguins have **molted** and grown new feathers for the winter.

The penguins find their partners.

When a penguin is three or four years old, it finds a partner at the rookery. The penguins stretch and bow to show each other they are ready to mate. The female penguin will lay her egg four weeks after mating.

Penguins need clean oceans.

Penguins feed on fish and other animals that live in the oceans. Oil and other garbage **pollute** oceans and kill the plants and animals in them. People can help by keeping the oceans clean.

Parts of a Penguin

Penguins are birds. Birds are covered with feathers and have their young by laying eggs. Most birds have wings and can fly, but penguins have flippers for swimming instead. Penguins are very good swimmers, but they cannot fly.

Feathers
Close together to keep
the penguin warm

Crop
Pocket in throat
used to store food

Bill
Sharp for catching fish
and squid

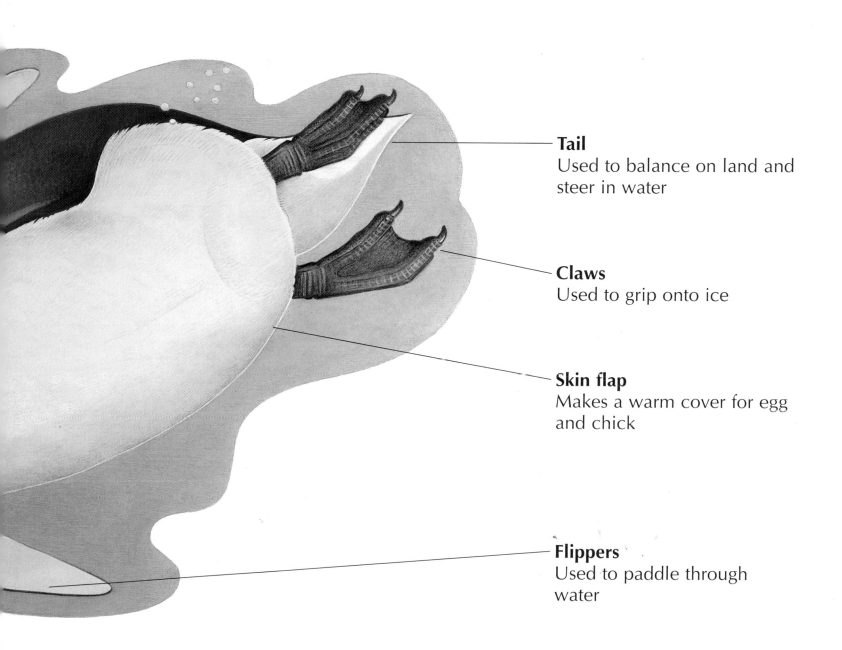

Tail
Used to balance on land and steer in water

Claws
Used to grip onto ice

Skin flap
Makes a warm cover for egg and chick

Flippers
Used to paddle through water

27

Other Antarctic Birds

The penguin in this book is an emperor penguin. Emperor penguins are the biggest and heaviest seabirds in the world. They grow to over 3 feet (1 m) high. Here are some other penguins and different kinds of birds that can be seen in Antarctica.

Adélie penguin

Rockhopper penguin

Chinstrap penguin

Sheathbill

Wandering
albatross

Great skua

Snow petrel

29

Where the Emperor Penguin Lives

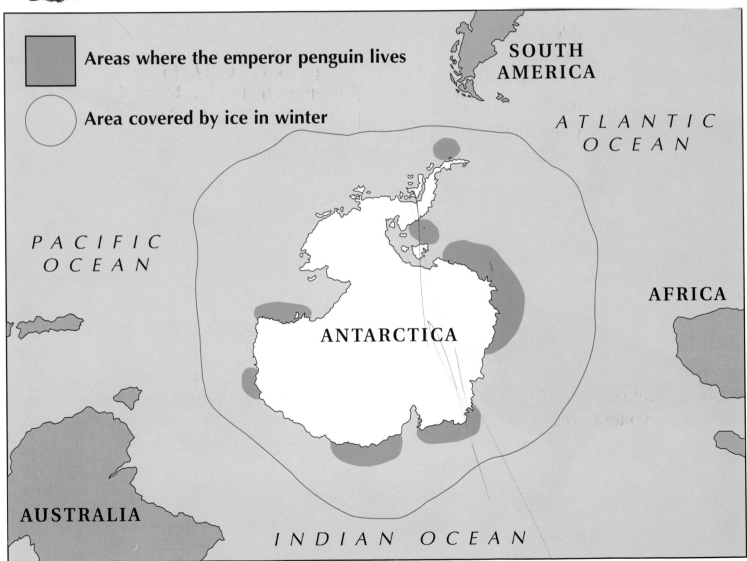

Areas where the emperor penguin lives

Area covered by ice in winter

SOUTH AMERICA

ATLANTIC OCEAN

PACIFIC OCEAN

AFRICA

ANTARCTICA

AUSTRALIA

INDIAN OCEAN

Glossary

Antarctica The area of land around the South Pole

Crop The pocket inside a penguin's throat used for storing food

Feeding ground The area where an animal goes to find its food

Hatch To come out of an egg

Molt To shed feathers before growing new ones

Pollute To poison something or make it dirty

Predator An animal that hunts and kills other animals for food

Prey To hunt or kill another animal for food

Rookery A place where birds gather together to breed

Squid A small sea animal with eight limbs and two tentacles

Index

Calling **11, 17**
Chick **10, 12–18**
Crop **13, 14, 26**
Diving **21**
Egg **5, 6, 8, 10, 24, 26**
Feathers **6, 17, 18, 20, 23, 26**
Feeding ground **19, 22**
Fish **7, 21, 25**
Flippers **26, 27**
Food **7, 8, 12, 13, 16, 19, 20**
Hatching **10**
Ice **5, 7, 10, 16**
Molting **23**
Ocean **5, 7, 8, 12, 15, 16, 19, 20**
Partner **24**
Pollution **25**
Predators **22**
Rookery **5, 7, 11, 12, 16, 19, 20, 23, 24**
Squid **7, 21**